Table Of Contents

Welcome

Out of the infinite things you could be doing at this exact moment, you chose to be here.

The fact that you are here is a testament to how pure and open your heart is to grow the love you have within yourself and for others. What a beautiful gift you are giving yourself, your partner, and the world we live in.

This intention you have to deepen your connection with your partner is rare in a world of superficiality. It is a treasure that cannot be forced or created, but only discovered and nurtured.

There is no end to how much you can nurture this love you have, and I am beyond grateful you have chosen this book as a guide to explore just how infinitely beautiful life can be when you devote it to deepening this feeling.

At the end of the day, that's all we want as humans, isn't it? To be seen, heard, understood, and to feel loved. We may desire external things, but they are all just a means to feel love.

What if we didn't need to rely on things outside of ourselves to feel this love inside of us?

The measure of fulfillment and joy in life doesn't come from what we have but from how we feel about ourselves and those around us. Although this book will help you grow your connection with your partner, it is also designed to help you deepen the relationship and love you have for yourself.

The depth of the love we have and can share with others is in direct proportion to the depth of love and connection we have for ourselves. This book will help you deepen both of those connections simultaneously because there is no separation between the two.

The more open, vulnerable, and compassionate you are with yourself, the more you are able to show the same toward your partner. We cannot pour from an empty cup, so we must fill ours first. The more we fill our cups, the more we can share with others.

How To Use The Journal

How To Answer The Questions

For every question in this journal, there will be a question, one page for your answer, and another page for your partner's answer. This is a joint journal, so it is designed for you both to complete together.

Each page will have a place for you to write your initials, so you know which answers are yours or your partner's.

One person will read the question out loud to the other partner and will write down the answer their partner gives. Whoever is sharing won't need to do anything other than share from a place of their own truth and be as open and honest as possible.

For the partner writing down the answers, it is best for that partner to suspend any judgment about the answers they hear and to hold space for their partner to feel as safe as possible.

This will allow for the most truthful answers to surface and a deeper connection to form through the shared vulnerability.

The more space and support you can offer your partner as they share their answers, the more likely they will show the same for you.

Underneath each journal question will be a list of follow-up questions to deepen the conversation. The next section of this book will go into more detail about them.

As you complete the journal, you'll likely think of additional questions you'd like to add. There are blank templates in the back of this book so that you can create your own and answer them in here.

It is highly recommended to add your own since every relationship is unique in its own way, so personalized questions will be vital to deepening your connection to each other.

Be Specific

For the person answering the question, be as specific as possible when sharing. Vague responses will make it hard for your partner to know exactly what you mean and what they can do to help.

Specificity creates clarity. The more clear and direct you are about what you're thinking, how you're feeling and why, the better your partner will be able to understand you.

Schedule A Specific Time Weekly

Schedule a time together weekly to answer a few questions until the journal is complete. This will help you both build a habit of deeply connecting with each other and will simultaneously serve as a time for you to be able to check in with each other to see how both of you are doing since the last journaling session together.

When you do this weekly, you will be able to see and feel the progress made with growing, nurturing, and deepening your connection to one another.

Reference This Journal Often

This journal isn't made for you both to fill it out once and put it away forever. It is designed to be a constantly updated, living, breathing documentation of how you both can love each other better.

This journal will be your best friend when you get into any disagreements. Whenever you get into conflict, remember to reference this journal. Think of it like your relationship bible. It will contain everything you need to know on how to heal your connection with your partner in their own words.

Follow-up Questions To Deepen Any Conversation & Connection

You can use these follow-up questions after any journal prompt you ask in this book to deepen the conversation, connection, and understanding of the other person.

I call these ***Connection Questions***.

These Connection Questions don't only apply to the journal questions, but to any conversation you have with anyone. When you ask them, you'll notice that your conversations will become deeper, richer, and more fulfilling than they ever have.

The questions in this journal will help you both find many answers that will allow you to create harmony more often, but the initial question or prompt is just the beginning.

Like in any conversation, if there was only one question and one answer between anyone you talked to, the relationship would not have much depth.

The relationship's depth is directly proportional to the depth you go within your conversations.

You learn infinitely more from questions than you do by giving answers. The initial question will help you get started, but where you will truly be able to understand your partner is in the follow-up Connection Questions you ask one another. Your goal is to be able to see the world the way they see it.

With every question you ask, you are breaking ground to create a deeper bond with your partner. Use any conflict as an invitation to become genuinely curious about your partner, what they're thinking, how they're feeling, and why.

Then whenever you ask a question, use these Connection Questions to create a safe space where your partner can open up to express how they are feeling. Enter their reality by asking them to explain what they mean and what makes them feel this way. This is how you create empathy and help them feel seen, heard, and understood.

Connection Question Examples

- What do you mean by that? or what do you mean by (insert the word or phrase they used that is vague)
- Tell me more.
- What's a specific example of what you mean?
- How does it make you feel?
- What makes you feel that way?
- How often does this happen? How often do you feel this way?
- Has it always been like this?
- When wasn't it like this?

Connection Questions are not limited to these examples at all. These are just a fraction of the infinite number that exists.

Connection Questions are any questions that take a conversation deeper. They typically have the person being asked to elaborate more on what they mean about what they just shared.

These questions allow both people to see parts of their partner that they haven't been able to see before and explore thoughts that their partner has not been conscious of. It is an enlightening and liberating experience for both people.

You'll know you're asking Connection Questions when the other person says things like, "Wow, I haven't thought about that before," or "I didn't know that's how I felt about it."

You'll know you're asking Connection Questions when the other person shares that they feel "lighter", more at ease, like a weight has been lifted off of their shoulders, or any sort of liberating emotion.

You can also check in at the end of the conversation to ask how they feel, and you will know whether you've helped them feel understood and seen by their answer. This is how you can gauge whether you are deepening your connection with your partner or not. Regular check-ins after conversations are vital to help you know if you both are growing your relationship.

Follow your curiosity and keep asking about what you don't quite understand or get the full picture of. The key to deepening any conversation and connection is by getting specific.

We tend to talk in vague phrases we think people understand, assuming others know how we think and feel. Most people don't have the same experiences and perspectives as us, so it is difficult for them to understand us immediately. We all do not have the same definition for the words we use, which is where much of the misunderstanding will come from.

For instance, support for one person may look like having a 3-hour-long conversation, while support for another person may be giving them a few hours alone to decompress.

This is why asking your partner clarification questions such as, "what do you mean by that?" will make a world of a difference in your connection with each other.

Remember, specificity creates clarity (and connection).

Ask the first question that pops into your mind. Follow your intuition on it. Go into the unknown and see what happens. The unknown is the only place where new possibilities can occur. There's no need to plan this out because you can't.

There's no way to know where a conversation will go, but as long as you continue to be truly curious about what your partner is thinking, feeling, and why, the outcome will be miraculous every single time.

The Cause Of Most Relationship Conflicts

Almost all challenges within a relationship boil down to one common denominator:

Communication

Conflict, judgment, and resentment within a relationship come from not knowing how our partner *truly* feels and **why**.

We tend to lash out, blame, criticize, and argue when we feel misunderstood.

Without communication, there can be no resolution.

Frustration perpetuates when we do not communicate with our partners.

Problems within a relationship dissolve when both partners can openly and vulnerably express their thoughts and feelings in a safe space without judging or blaming one another.

Once a person feels seen, heard, and understood, feelings of love, harmony, and joy are inevitable. At that point, the problem no longer exists, or a simple solution emerges from the clarity of understanding each other's perspectives.

Discomfort Deepens Relationships

It will be uncomfortable to break the pattern of judgment during a conflict with our partner and replace it with curiosity. That is how any new habit works, but as with all things with discomfort, that is how we grow.

When we are exercising, the discomfort never really goes away. We learn to accept it as a part of the natural growing process and that it is okay.

This is how we can also view having uncomfortable conversations. Once you normalize uncomfortable conversations, committing to having them regularly becomes much easier, and growth becomes a natural byproduct within your relationship.

If we are not feeling discomfort during a workout, we will not grow. The same is true for our relationships. If we are not having uncomfortable conversations, our relationships won't grow.

Although it feels wonderful making joyful memories with our partner, that only creates breadth, which is just one dimension of a partnership.

Uncomfortable conversations allow us to deepen our connection with each other and create depth that makes a relationship immensely fulfilling.

In relationships, pleasure creates breadth. Discomfort creates depth.

Both are required to create a holistic, healthy partnership.

Partners that focus solely on creating pleasurable memories are easily perishable because they do not have strong roots. They may have a wide breadth of happy experiences but lack the depth of deep roots within each other's hearts that can weather any storm.

The cost of having uncomfortable conversations is our ego.

What we gain is a beautiful, harmonious, and joyful lifelong, fulfilling partnership with infinite dimensions and love for us to discover.

How To Deepen The Connection With Your Partner

One of the best ways to deepen your connection to anything in life, especially your relationships, is by being truly curious.

When you inevitably get into disagreements with your partner, change your reaction to becoming genuinely curious about what they are thinking, why, what made them develop this perspective, and how they're feeling.

Replace each judgment with a question from a place of pure curiosity to understand what your partner is experiencing and why.

Enter their reality and see how they see the world. Then you will understand why they feel the way they do. That is what creates connection and harmony. This is where the magic happens.

With that simple shift, you will be able to prevent most disagreements from becoming destructive, de-escalate them quickly, and come to understand your partner more.

Every conflict is an opportunity to deepen your connection with your partner. Disagreements bring up blind spots both of you have not seen before, allowing you to understand each other better.

Disagreements are not the problem – how we handle them is. There's no need to try to avoid them, as they are inevitable. Disagreements are inherently natural and neutral, but they can either destroy or deepen our relationships.

The outcome of each one depends on whether we choose to be curious or to be right.

Most couples' goal in a disagreement is to be right – this is how most relationships are slowly destroyed from the inside out.

When you change your goal within each conversation from wanting to be right to wanting to understand your partner better, conflict melts, and love resurfaces.

When we don't ask questions, we assume we know what our partner means, when most of the time, we don't because we are not them.

We do not have the same experience, personality, thought processes, and beliefs as our partners, so how can we possibly assume we know what they are experiencing?

It is assumptions that cause conflicts within our relationships.

Assumptions create judgment and disconnection.

Curiosity creates connection. The root of understanding is curiosity.

When a disagreement arises, you can break the pattern of the conflict by taking a few deep breaths to ground yourself and asking yourself this one question:

How can I help my partner feel seen, safe, and understood right now?

Once you can regulate your nervous system and get out of a state of fight or flight by taking deep breaths, the answer will become clear to you as to what you can do to create harmony again.

If things are still unclear to you, this is the perfect time to ask questions from a place of genuine curiosity to gain a better understanding of what your partner is thinking and feeling.

It only takes one partner to begin the momentum of creating peace, but it is exponentially more effective and powerful when both partners are actively practicing helping each other feel seen, safe, and understood.

The Framework For Creating Compassionate Communication

We've covered quite a bit on the philosophy behind resolving conflicts and creating a deeper connection with your partner, but it has not been orchestrated into a concise, organized, and actionable process yet.

Trying to remember everything that you just read during a real-time conflict would be difficult, so I've summarized everything you just read into a simple, memorable framework on how to understand and connect with your partner through what I call ***Compassionate Communication***.

Compassionate Communication Framework

Help your partner feel safe to lay all their cards on the **T.A.B.L.E.** and share what they're thinking and feeling

T - Take deep breaths

Ground yourself in the present moment and regulate your emotions by taking deep breaths. Getting out of a fight or flight state is vital for creating a safe space where you both can share how you both feel.

A - Ask specific questions

Help your partner get specific with what they are feeling and why by asking questions from a place of curiosity and love. Questions create space for your partner to hear their own thought process to understand themselves better. Questions are the doorway to understanding. A good rule of thumb when you are holding space for your partner is to let 80% of your dialogue be questions, and 20% be responses to what they say. Follow your intuition on what questions to ask.

B - Be truly curious

Become truly curious about what your partner is thinking, what they are feeling, and why. Seek to understand where they are coming from. Let your curiosity lead the conversation.

L - Listen without judgment or an agenda

Suspend all judgment when listening to your partner. Don't listen to respond. Don't listen to give advice. Listen without an agenda. You can either be in harmony or be right. Truly listening to your partner means letting go of judging what they are saying and needing to be right. This allows you to truly hear what they are saying to help them feel seen, heard, understood, and loved.

E - Enter their reality

The way to empathize with your partner is by asking questions so you can enter their reality. By doing this, you can see the world the way they see it and discover why they think the way they do. This is the foundation of understanding your partner and connecting with them on a deeper level than ever before.

Journal Questions

Date:

“Opening up a conversation can be opening up a world of new possibilities.”

— Michelle Lederman

When do you feel most like your true self?

Connection Question Examples: What do you mean by that? Tell me more.
Can you share an example of this? What makes you feel that way?

Initials:

When do you feel most like your true self?

Connection Question Examples: What do you mean by that? Tell me more. Can you share an example of this? What makes you feel that way?

Initials:

“I define connection as the energy that exists between people when they feel seen, heard, and valued; when they can give and receive without judgment; and when they derive sustenance and strength from the relationship.”

— Brené Brown

What are your favorite ways for me to show you that I love you?

Connection Question Examples: What do you mean by that? Tell me more. Can you share an example of this? What makes you feel that way?

Initials:

What are your favorite ways for me to show you that I love you?

Connection Question Examples: What do you mean by that? Tell me more. Can you share an example of this? What makes you feel that way?

Initials:

"The strongest love is the love that can demonstrate its fragility."

— Paulo Coelho

What are the first 3 words or phrases that pop into your mind when you think of me?

Connection Question Examples: What do you mean by that? Tell me more. Can you share an example of this? What makes you feel that way?

Initials:

What are the first 3 words or phrases that pop into your mind when you think of me?

Connection Question Examples: What do you mean by that? Tell me more. Can you share an example of this? What makes you feel that way?

Initials:

"Love is about bottomless empathy, born out of the heart's revelation that another person is every bit as real as you are."

— Jonathan Franzen

What do we do that tends to deepen our connection and love for each other? What are some ways we can do that more often?

Connection Question Examples: What do you mean by that? Tell me more. Can you share an example of this? What makes you feel that way?

Initials:

What do we do that tends to deepen our connection and love for each other? What are some ways we can do that more often?

Connection Question Examples: What do you mean by that? Tell me more.
Can you share an example of this? What makes you feel that way?

Initials:

"We think we listen, but very rarely do we listen with real understanding, true empathy. Yet listening, of this very special kind, is one of the most potent forces for change that I know."

— Carl Rogers

What are your priorities in life right now, and how would you rank them?

Connection Question Examples: What do you mean by that? Tell me more. Can you share an example of this? What makes you feel that way?

Initials:

What are your priorities in life right now, and how would you rank them?

Connection Question Examples: What do you mean by that? Tell me more. Can you share an example of this? What makes you feel that way?

Initials:

"Love someone exactly as they are, and they'll transform into the best possible version of who they could be.

Love yourself exactly as you are, and you will do the same."

— Brianna Wiest

What can I do to help you feel safe?

Connection Question Examples: What do you mean by that? Tell me more. Can you share an example of this? What makes you feel that way?

Initials:

What can I do to help you feel safe?

Connection Question Examples: What do you mean by that? Tell me more. Can you share an example of this? What makes you feel that way?

Initials:

“Empathy has no script. There is no right way or wrong way to do it.

It’s simply listening, holding space, withholding judgment, emotionally connecting, and communicating that incredibly healing message of ‘You’re not alone.’”

— Brené Brown

What is your idea of a healthy relationship? List everything you can think of.

Connection Question Examples: What do you mean by that? Tell me more. Can you share an example of this? What makes you feel that way?

Initials:

What is your idea of a healthy relationship? List everything you can think of.

Connection Question Examples: What do you mean by that? Tell me more.
Can you share an example of this? What makes you feel that way?

Initials:

“The most important thing in communication is to hear what isn’t being said.”

— Peter Drucker

If you could summarize in one sentence something for me to remember for how to help you feel safe, understood, and loved, what would that be?

Connection Question Examples: What do you mean by that? Tell me more. Can you share an example of this? What makes you feel that way?

Initials:

If you could summarize in one sentence something for me to remember for how to help you feel safe, understood, and loved, what would that be?

Connection Question Examples: What do you mean by that? Tell me more. Can you share an example of this? What makes you feel that way?

Initials:

“Emotional pain cannot kill you, but running from it can.

Allow. Embrace. Let yourself feel. Let yourself heal.”

— Vironika Tugaleva

When you are frustrated, do you usually want a solution or support? To you, what's the difference between them? How will I know when you want one or the other?

Connection Question Examples: What do you mean by that? Tell me more. Can you share an example of this? What makes you feel that way?

Initials:

When you are frustrated, do you usually want a solution or support? To you, what's the difference between them? How will I know when you want one or the other?

Connection Question Examples: What do you mean by that? Tell me more. Can you share an example of this? What makes you feel that way?

Initials:

"Love without attachment is the purest love because it isn't about what others can give you because you're empty.

It is about what you can give others because you're already full."

— Yasmin Mogahed

What does support look like to you specifically? Can you give me an example?

Connection Question Examples: What do you mean by that? Tell me more. Can you share an example of this? What makes you feel that way?

Initials:

What does support look like to you specifically? Can you give me an example?

Connection Question Examples: What do you mean by that? Tell me more. Can you share an example of this? What makes you feel that way?

Initials:

“We must learn to regard people less in the light of what they do or omit to do, and more in the light of what they suffer.”

— Dietrich Bonhoeffer,
Letters and Papers from Prison

When do you usually feel closest to me?

Connection Question Examples: What do you mean by that? Tell me more. Can you share an example of this? What makes you feel that way?

Initials:

When do you usually feel closest to me?

Connection Question Examples: What do you mean by that? Tell me more. Can you share an example of this? What makes you feel that way?

Initials:

“Don’t give up at the first signs of friction: Only through clear communication, flexibility, and willingness to adapt can you find a relationship that will weather the storms of life.”

— Tom Miles

How do you usually work through your own problems?

Connection Question Examples: What do you mean by that? Tell me more. Can you share an example of this? What makes you feel that way?

Initials:

How do you usually work through your own problems?

Connection Question Examples: What do you mean by that? Tell me more. Can you share an example of this? What makes you feel that way?

Initials:

"People cry, not because they're weak.

It's because they've been strong for too long."

— Johnny Depp

When you are stressed, what is your initial reaction to it? How do you usually cope with it?

Connection Question Examples: What do you mean by that? Tell me more. Can you share an example of this? What makes you feel that way?

Initials:

When you are stressed, what is your initial reaction to it? How do you usually cope with it?

Connection Question Examples: What do you mean by that? Tell me more. Can you share an example of this? What makes you feel that way?

Initials:

"A lot of problems in the world would be solved if we talked to each other instead of about each other."

— Nicky Gumbel

When do you feel most expansive and alive?

Connection Question Examples: What do you mean by that? Tell me more.
Can you share an example of this? What makes you feel that way?

Initials:

When do you feel most expansive and alive?

Connection Question Examples: What do you mean by that? Tell me more.
Can you share an example of this? What makes you feel that way?

Initials:

“Vulnerability sounds like truth and feels like courage.

Truth and courage aren't always comfortable, but they're never weakness.”

— Brené Brown

When you are stressed and overwhelmed, how do you usually want me to help?

Connection Question Examples: What do you mean by that? Tell me more. Can you share an example of this? What makes you feel that way?

Initials:

When you are stressed and overwhelmed, how do you usually want me to help?

Connection Question Examples: What do you mean by that? Tell me more. Can you share an example of this? What makes you feel that way?

Initials:

"To effectively communicate, we must realize that we are all different in the way we perceive the world and use this understanding as a guide to our communication with others."

— Tony Robbins

After you've had a long, stressful day, what do you usually want?

Connection Question Examples: What do you mean by that? Tell me more. Can you share an example of this? What makes you feel that way?

Initials:

After you've had a long, stressful day, what do you usually want?

Connection Question Examples: What do you mean by that? Tell me more. Can you share an example of this? What makes you feel that way?

Initials:

“Every act of communication is a miracle of translation.”

— Ken Liu

What is your favorite way to express your creativity? Or what are your favorite means of creative self-expression?

Connection Question Examples: What do you mean by that? Tell me more. Can you share an example of this? What makes you feel that way?

Initials:

What is your favorite way to express your creativity? Or what are your favorite means of creative self-expression?

Connection Question Examples: What do you mean by that? Tell me more. Can you share an example of this? What makes you feel that way?

Initials:

“Empathy doesn't require that we have the exact same experiences as the person sharing their story with us...

Empathy is connecting with the emotion that someone is experiencing, not the event or the circumstance.”

— Brené Brown

When we get into disagreements or conflicts, to you, what would be the best way for us to create harmony again? Create an ideal step-by-step process.

Connection Question Examples: What do you mean by that? Tell me more. Can you share an example of this? What makes you feel that way?

Initials:

When we get into disagreements or conflicts, to you, what would be the best way for us to create harmony again? Create an ideal step-by-step process.

Connection Question Examples: What do you mean by that? Tell me more. Can you share an example of this? What makes you feel that way?

Initials:

"Speak from your heart to their heart instead of from your mind to their mind."

— Rori Raye

What makes you feel seen, heard, and understood?

Connection Question Examples: What do you mean by that? Tell me more. Can you share an example of this? What makes you feel that way?

Initials:

What makes you feel seen, heard, and understood?

Connection Question Examples: What do you mean by that? Tell me more. Can you share an example of this? What makes you feel that way?

Initials:

"Vulnerability is the birthplace of love, belonging, joy, courage, empathy, and creativity. It is the source of hope, empathy, accountability, and authenticity. If we want greater clarity in our purpose or deeper and more meaningful spiritual lives, vulnerability is the path."

— Brené Brown

What makes things worse when we are in conflict?

Connection Question Examples: What do you mean by that? Tell me more. Can you share an example of this? What makes you feel that way?

Initials:

What makes things worse when we are in conflict?

Connection Question Examples: What do you mean by that? Tell me more. Can you share an example of this? What makes you feel that way?

Initials:

“When we feel love and kindness toward others, it not only makes others feel loved and cared for, but it also helps us to develop inner happiness and peace.”

— 14th Dalai Lama

What makes things better when we are in conflict?

Connection Question Examples: What do you mean by that? Tell me more. Can you share an example of this? What makes you feel that way?

Initials:

What makes things better when we are in conflict?

Connection Question Examples: What do you mean by that? Tell me more. Can you share an example of this? What makes you feel that way?

Initials:

“Deep human connection is the purpose and the result of a meaningful life – and it will inspire the most amazing acts of love, generosity, and humanity.”

— Melinda Gates

When are you happiest?

Connection Question Examples: What do you mean by that? Tell me more. Can you share an example of this? What makes you feel that way?

Initials:

When are you happiest?

Connection Question Examples: What do you mean by that? Tell me more. Can you share an example of this? What makes you feel that way?

Initials:

“You have to make a space in your heart, in your mind, and in your life itself for authentic human connection.”

— Marianne Williamson

When do you feel most at peace?

Connection Question Examples: What do you mean by that? Tell me more. Can you share an example of this? What makes you feel that way?

Initials:

When do you feel most at peace?

Connection Question Examples: What do you mean by that? Tell me more.
Can you share an example of this? What makes you feel that way?

Initials:

“Trust is earned in the smallest of moments.

It is earned not through heroic deeds, or even highly visible actions, but through paying attention, listening, and gestures of genuine care and connection.”

— Brené Brown

What makes you feel guilty to ask for from me and why?

Connection Question Examples: What do you mean by that? Tell me more. Can you share an example of this? What makes you feel that way?

Initials:

What makes you feel guilty to ask for from me and why?

Connection Question Examples: What do you mean by that? Tell me more. Can you share an example of this? What makes you feel that way?

Initials:

“Communication to a relationship is like oxygen is to life. Without it, it dies.”

— Tony A. Gaskins Jr.

When are you usually afraid to tell me something? What makes you afraid to tell me? How can I help you not be as afraid to tell me?

Connection Question Examples: What do you mean by that? Tell me more.
Can you share an example of this? What makes you feel that way?

Initials:

When are you usually afraid to tell me something? What makes you afraid to tell me? How can I help you not be as afraid to tell me?

Connection Question Examples: What do you mean by that? Tell me more.
Can you share an example of this? What makes you feel that way?

Initials:

“To the extent that our experience of suffering reminds us of what everyone else also endures, it serves as a powerful inspiration to practice compassion and avoid causing others pain.”

— Dalai Lama

What makes you feel like a kid again?

Connection Question Examples: What do you mean by that? Tell me more. Can you share an example of this? What makes you feel that way?

Initials:

What makes you feel like a kid again?

Connection Question Examples: What do you mean by that? Tell me more. Can you share an example of this? What makes you feel that way?

Initials:

"You never really understand a person until you consider things from [their] point of view… until you climb into [their] skin and walk around in it."

— Harper Lee

When we see something in each other that we would like to change, what is the best way to address it?

Connection Question Examples: What do you mean by that? Tell me more. Can you share an example of this? What makes you feel that way?

Initials:

When we see something in each other that we would like to change, what is the best way to address it?

Connection Question Examples: What do you mean by that? Tell me more. Can you share an example of this? What makes you feel that way?

Initials:

“When I get ready to talk to people, I spend two-thirds of the time thinking what they want to hear and one-third thinking about what I want to say.”

— Abraham Lincoln

How can we talk about what we disagree on without getting into heated arguments?

Connection Question Examples: What do you mean by that? Tell me more. Can you share an example of this? What makes you feel that way?

Initials:

How can we talk about what we disagree on without getting into heated arguments?

Connection Question Examples: What do you mean by that? Tell me more. Can you share an example of this? What makes you feel that way?

Initials:

“Empathy isn’t just listening, it’s asking the questions whose answers need to be listened to. Empathy requires knowing you know nothing.

Empathy means acknowledging a horizon of context that extends perpetually beyond what you can see.”

— Leslie Jamison

What makes you happy to see me do for myself?

Connection Question Examples: What do you mean by that? Tell me more. Can you share an example of this? What makes you feel that way?

Initials:

What makes you happy to see me do for myself?

Connection Question Examples: What do you mean by that? Tell me more. Can you share an example of this? What makes you feel that way?

Initials:

"If you love a flower, don't pick it up. Because if you pick it up, it dies, and it ceases to be what you love.

So, if you love a flower, let it be. Love is not about possession. Love is about appreciation."

— Rajneesh

How can we create a safe space for us to be truly open and feel like we can share anything with each other more often?

Connection Question Examples: What do you mean by that? Tell me more.
Can you share an example of this? What makes you feel that way?

Initials:

How can we create a safe space for us to be truly open and feel like we can share anything with each other more often?

Connection Question Examples: What do you mean by that? Tell me more. Can you share an example of this? What makes you feel that way?

Initials:

“We have two ears and one mouth so that we can listen twice as much as we speak.”

— Epictetus

When do you feel most comfortable around me?

Connection Question Examples: What do you mean by that? Tell me more.
Can you share an example of this? What makes you feel that way?

Initials:

When do you feel most comfortable around me?

Connection Question Examples: What do you mean by that? Tell me more.
Can you share an example of this? What makes you feel that way?

Initials:

“What happens when people open their hearts?

They get better.”

— Haruki Murakami

What would make you want to put off bringing up something that could affect our relationship? How does putting it off affect the relationship? How can I help you feel safe to bring it up?

Connection Question Examples: What do you mean by that? Tell me more. Can you share an example of this? What makes you feel that way?

Initials:

What would make you want to put off bringing up something that could affect our relationship? How does putting it off affect the relationship? How can I help you feel safe to bring it up?

Connection Question Examples: What do you mean by that? Tell me more. Can you share an example of this? What makes you feel that way?

Initials:

“Love someone because their soul inspires you, not because you’re interested in the relief from loneliness and companionship they can provide. Anybody can do that.

Not just anybody can show you to yourself.”

— Brianna Wiest

How did you know when you truly loved me for the first time?

Connection Question Examples: What do you mean by that? Tell me more. Can you share an example of this? What makes you feel that way?

Initials:

How did you know when you truly loved me for the first time?

Connection Question Examples: What do you mean by that? Tell me more.
Can you share an example of this? What makes you feel that way?

Initials:

Create Your Own Questions

Connection Question Examples: What do you mean by that? Tell me more. Can you share an example of this? What makes you feel that way?

Initials:

Connection Question Examples: What do you mean by that? Tell me more. Can you share an example of this? What makes you feel that way?

Initials:

Connection Question Examples: What do you mean by that? Tell me more. Can you share an example of this? What makes you feel that way?

Initials:

Connection Question Examples: What do you mean by that? Tell me more. Can you share an example of this? What makes you feel that way?

Initials:

Connection Question Examples: What do you mean by that? Tell me more. Can you share an example of this? What makes you feel that way?

Initials:

Connection Question Examples: What do you mean by that? Tell me more. Can you share an example of this? What makes you feel that way?

Initials:

Connection Question Examples: What do you mean by that? Tell me more. Can you share an example of this? What makes you feel that way?

Initials:

Connection Question Examples: What do you mean by that? Tell me more. Can you share an example of this? What makes you feel that way?

Initials:

Connection Question Examples: What do you mean by that? Tell me more. Can you share an example of this? What makes you feel that way?

Initials:

Connection Question Examples: What do you mean by that? Tell me more. Can you share an example of this? What makes you feel that way?

Initials:

Connection Question Examples: What do you mean by that? Tell me more. Can you share an example of this? What makes you feel that way?

Initials:

Connection Question Examples: What do you mean by that? Tell me more. Can you share an example of this? What makes you feel that way?

Initials:

Connection Question Examples: What do you mean by that? Tell me more. Can you share an example of this? What makes you feel that way?

Initials:

Connection Question Examples: What do you mean by that? Tell me more. Can you share an example of this? What makes you feel that way?

Initials:

Connection Question Examples: What do you mean by that? Tell me more. Can you share an example of this? What makes you feel that way?

Initials:

Connection Question Examples: What do you mean by that? Tell me more. Can you share an example of this? What makes you feel that way?

Initials:

Connection Question Examples: What do you mean by that? Tell me more. Can you share an example of this? What makes you feel that way?

Initials:

Connection Question Examples: What do you mean by that? Tell me more.
Can you share an example of this? What makes you feel that way?

Initials:

Connection Question Examples: What do you mean by that? Tell me more. Can you share an example of this? What makes you feel that way?

Initials:

Connection Question Examples: What do you mean by that? Tell me more. Can you share an example of this? What makes you feel that way?

Initials:

Connection Question Examples: What do you mean by that? Tell me more. Can you share an example of this? What makes you feel that way?

Initials:

Connection Question Examples: What do you mean by that? Tell me more. Can you share an example of this? What makes you feel that way?

Initials:

Connection Question Examples: What do you mean by that? Tell me more. Can you share an example of this? What makes you feel that way?

Initials:

Connection Question Examples: What do you mean by that? Tell me more. Can you share an example of this? What makes you feel that way?

Initials:

Connection Question Examples: What do you mean by that? Tell me more. Can you share an example of this? What makes you feel that way?

Initials:

Connection Question Examples: What do you mean by that? Tell me more. Can you share an example of this? What makes you feel that way?

Initials:

Connection Question Examples: What do you mean by that? Tell me more. Can you share an example of this? What makes you feel that way?

Initials:

Connection Question Examples: What do you mean by that? Tell me more. Can you share an example of this? What makes you feel that way?

Initials:

Connection Question Examples: What do you mean by that? Tell me more. Can you share an example of this? What makes you feel that way?

Initials:

Connection Question Examples: What do you mean by that? Tell me more. Can you share an example of this? What makes you feel that way?

Initials:

Connection Question Examples: What do you mean by that? Tell me more. Can you share an example of this? What makes you feel that way?

Initials:

Connection Question Examples: What do you mean by that? Tell me more. Can you share an example of this? What makes you feel that way?

Initials:

Connection Question Examples: What do you mean by that? Tell me more. Can you share an example of this? What makes you feel that way?

Initials:

Connection Question Examples: What do you mean by that? Tell me more. Can you share an example of this? What makes you feel that way?

Initials:

Connection Question Examples: What do you mean by that? Tell me more. Can you share an example of this? What makes you feel that way?

Initials:

Connection Question Examples: What do you mean by that? Tell me more. Can you share an example of this? What makes you feel that way?

Initials:

Connection Question Examples: What do you mean by that? Tell me more. Can you share an example of this? What makes you feel that way?

Initials:

Connection Question Examples: What do you mean by that? Tell me more. Can you share an example of this? What makes you feel that way?

Initials:

Connection Question Examples: What do you mean by that? Tell me more. Can you share an example of this? What makes you feel that way?

Initials:

Connection Question Examples: What do you mean by that? Tell me more.
Can you share an example of this? What makes you feel that way?

Initials:

Other books by Joseph Nguyen

Don't Believe Everything You Think: Why Your Thinking Is The Beginning & End Of Suffering

Beyond Thoughts: An Exploration Of Who We Are Beyond Our Minds

For more resources, guides, and books, you may visit:
www.josephnguyen.org

ISBN: 979-8-9864065-5-8

First printing edition 2022 in United States

Printed in Poland
by Amazon Fulfillment
Poland Sp. z o.o., Wrocław

43813280R00115